THE
POCKET
PRONUNCIATION
GUIDE
TO
BIBLE PEOPLE,
PLACES, *and* THINGS

David C Cook®
transforming lives together

THE POCKET PRONUNCIATION GUIDE
TO BIBLE PEOPLE, PLACES, AND THINGS
Published by David C Cook
4050 Lee Vance Drive
Colorado Springs, CO 80918 U.S.A.

David C Cook U.K., Kingsway Communications
Eastbourne, East Sussex BN23 6NT, England

The graphic circle C logo is a registered
trademark of David C Cook.

LCCN 2017933738
ISBN 978-1-4347-1160-1

© 2017 David C Cook

The Team: Matt Lockhart, Nick Lee,
Abby DeBenedittis, Julie Neddo, Susan Murdock
Cover Design: Amy Konyndyk
Cover Photo: Getty Images

Printed in the United States of America

First Edition 2017

1 2 3 4 5 6 7 8 9 10

022817

Introduction

*Do your best to present yourself to
God as one approved, a worker who
does not need to be ashamed and who
correctly handles the word of truth.*

2 Timothy 2:15

Whether you are a first-time Bible
teacher or a long-serving pro, this handy
pronunciation guide is a helpful tool
when preparing to teach and encourage
others with God's Word. Adapted from
the popular "How to Say It" feature
from the bestselling *Standard Lesson
Commentary*, this resource equips you
in a very practical way by providing
pronunciation help for difficult-to-say
words that come up in Sunday school
lessons, sermons, and Bible studies.

In this resource, you will find an alphabetical listing of over 1,200 of the most often mispronounced words in the Bible. This easy-to-use guide puts Bible words in a single column, along with the phonetic spelling of the words so that you can pronounce difficult-to-say Bible words accurately and confidently.

Sometimes a word will include a notation of an alternate spelling. There are times in Scripture that the same person may have a name that is spelled in different ways. For example, Jephthae, the judge, is also known as Jephthah. Sometimes the two different spellings reflect slight differences in the original Hebrew, and so the translations generally try to reflect those differences. Also, the different manuscripts on which the translations are based sometimes have different readings. Thus, one translation may have "Jephthae" and another "Jephthah" in the same passage.

Because of these differences in translations, on occasion a pronunciation in this guide will cite a particular Bible version, either the King James Version (KJV) or the New International Version (NIV).

Our prayer is that this practical guide will help you be prepared as you teach and encourage others with God's Word. May God bless your efforts in sharing the Bible well and accurately.

— Aa —

Aaron: *Air*-un.

Aaronic: Air-*ahn*-ik.

Abaddon: Uh-*bad*-dun.

Abana: *Ab*-uh-nuh or Uh-*ban*-uh.

Abba: *Ab*-buh.

Abdeel: *Ab*-dee-el.

Abdon: *Ab*-don.

Abednego: Uh-*bed*-nee-go.

Abel-meholah: *Ay*-buhl-muh-***ho***-lah.

Abi: *Ay*-bye.

Abiah: Uh-*bye*-uh.

Abiathar: Uh-*bye*-uh-thar.

Abib: *Ay*-bib.

Abiel: *Ay*-be-el.

Abiezrite: *Ay*-bye-***ez***-rite.

Abihu: Uh-*bye*-hew.

Abijah: Uh-*bye*-juh.

Abilene: *Ab*-ih-leen or Ab-ih-*lee*-neh.

Abimelech or Abimelek: Uh-*bim*-eh-lek.

Abinadab: Uh-*bin*-uh-dab.

Abinoam: Uh-*bin*-oh-am.

Abishag: *Ab*-ih-shag.

Abishai: Uh-*bish*-ay-eye.

Abishalom: Uh-*bish*-uh-lum.

Abraham: *Ay*-bruh-ham.

Abrahamic: Ay-bruh-*ham*-ik.

Abram: *Ay*-brum.

Absalom: *Ab*-suh-lum.

abyss: uh-*bis*.

acacia: uh-*kay*-shuh.

Acbor: *Ak*-bor.

Accho (KJV): *Ak*-oh.

Achaia: Uh-*kay*-uh.

Achan: *Ay*-kan.

Achbor: *Ak*-bor.

Achish: *Ay*-kish.

Achmetha: Ock-*me*-thuh.

Achor: *Ah*-core.

Acropolis: Uh-*krop*-uh-lis.

Adaiah: Add-uh-*eye*-uh or Ah-*day*-yuh.

Adamah: Ad-uh-*mah*.

Adar: *Ay*-dar.

Adhem: *Ah*-dem.

Admah: *Ad*-muh.

Adonijah: Ad-oh-*nye*-juh.

Adoram: Uh-*doe*-rum.

Adramyttium: Ad-ruh-*mitt*-ee-um.

Adriatic: Ay-dree-*at*-ic.

Adullam: Ah-*dull*-um.

Aegean: Uh-*jee*-un.

Aeneas: Ee-*nee*-us.

Agabus: *Ag*-uh-bus.

Agag: *Ay*-gag.

Agagite: *Ay*-guh-gite.

agora: *ag*-uh-ruh.

Agrippa: Uh-*grip*-puh.

Agur: *Ay*-gur.

Ahab: *Ay*-hab.

Ahasuerus (KJV): Uh-haz-you-*ee*-rus.

Ahava: Uh-*hay*-vuh.

Ahaz: *Ay*-haz.

Ahaziah: Ay-huh-*zye*-uh.

Ahijah: Uh-*hi*-juh.

Ahikam: Uh-*hi*-kum.

Ahilud: Uh-*hi*-lud.

Ahimelech or Ahimelek: Uh-*him*-eh-leck.

Ahinoam: Uh-*hin*-oh-um.

Ahisamach: Uh-*his*-ah-mak.

Ahithophel: Uh-*hith*-oh-fel.

Ahitub: Uh-*hi*-tub.

Aholiab: Uh-*ho*-lih-ab.

Ahuzzath: Uh-*huz*-uth.

Ai: *Ay*-eye.

Akhisar: Ahk-iss-*ar*.

Akko (NIV): *Ak*-oh.

Akkub: *Ak*-ub.

alabaster: *al*-uh-*bas*-ter.

Alashehir: *Al*-uh-shuh-***here***.

Alexander: Al-iks-*an*-der.

Alexandria: Al-iks-*an*-dree-uh.

Alexandrians: Al-iks-*an*-dree-unz.

Alpha: *Al*-fuh.

Alphaeus: Al-*fee*-us.

Amalek: *Am*-uh-lek.

Amalekites: *Am*-uh-leh-kites or Uh-*mal*-
   ih-kites.

Amariah: *Am*-uh-***rye***-uh.

Amaziah: Am-uh-*zye*-uh.

ambassage (KJV): *am*-buh-sij.

amethyst: *am*-uh-thust.

Amittai: Uh-*mit*-eye.

Amminadab: Uh-*min*-uh-dab.

Ammon: *Am*-mun.

Ammonites: *Am*-mun-ites.

Amnon: *Am*-nun.

Amon: *Ay*-mun.

Amorites: *Am*-uh-rites.

Amos: *Ay*-mus.

Amoz: *Ay*-mahz.

Amphipolis: Am-*fip*-oh-liss.

Amram: *Am*-ram.

Anaiah: Uh-*nye*-uh.

Anak: *Ay*-nak.

Anakims (KJV): *An*-uh-kims.

Anakites (NIV): An-uh-kites.

Ananias: An-uh-*nye*-us.

Anath: *Ay*-nath.

Anathoth: *An*-uh-thoth.

Andrew: *An*-drew.

Andronicus: *An*-dro-**nye**-kus.

Annas: *An*-nus.

Antioch: *An*-tee-ock.

Antiochus: An-*tie*-oh-kus.

Antipas: *An*-tih-pus.

Antipater: An-*tih*-puh-ter.

Apharsachites: Uh-*far*-sak-ites.

Apharsathchites: Af-ar-*sath*-kits.

Aphiah: Uh-*fye*-uh.

Aphrodite: Af-ruh-*dite*-ee.

Apollo: Uh-*pah*-lo.

Apollonia: Ap-uh-*lo*-nee-uh.

Apollos: Uh-*pahl*-us.

apostolic: ap-uh-*stahl*-ick.

Apphia: *Af*-ee-uh-or *Ap*-fee-uh.

Appii (KJV): *Ap*-pie-eye.

Appius (NIV): *Ap*-pea-us.

Aqaba: *Ock*-uh-buh.

Aquila: *Ack*-wih-luh.

Arabia: Uh-*ray*-bee-uh.

Arabian: Uh-*ray*-bee-un.

Aram: *Air*-um.

Aramaic: *Air*-uh-***may***-ik.

Arameans (NIV): *Ar*-uh-***me***-uns.

Aratus: *Air*-uh-tus.

Araunah: Uh-*raw*-nuh.

Archelaus: Ar-kuh-*lay*-us.

Archippus: Ar-*kip*-us.

Arcturus: Ark-*tour*-us.

Areopagite: Air-ee-*op*-uh-gite (*g* as in *get*).

Areopagus: Air-ee-*op*-uh-gus.

Aretas: *Air*-ih-tas.

Arimathaea or Arimathea: *Air*-uh-muh-
   thee-uh (*th* as in *thin*).

Aristarchus: Air-iss-*tar*-cuss.

Aristobulus: Uh-*ris*-toe-***bew***-lus.

Armageddon: Ar-muh-*ged*-un.

Armenia: Ar-*me*-nee-uh.

Arnon: *Ar*-non.

Aroer: Uh-*ro*-er.

Artaxerxes: Ar-tuh-*zerk*-seez.

Artemis: *Ar*-teh-miss.

Asa: *Ay*-suh.

Asahiah: As-uh-*hi*-uh.

Asaph: *Ay*-saff.

ascension: uh-*sen(t)*-shun.

Asenath: *As*-eh-nath.

Aser: *A*-ser (*A* as in *had*).

Ashdod: *Ash*-dod.

Ashdodites: *Ash*-duh-dites.

Asher: *Ash*-er.

Asherah: Uh-*she*-ruh.

Ashkelon: *Ash*-keh-lon or *As*-keh-lon.

Ashpenaz: *Ash*-pih-naz.

Ashtaroth: *Ash*-tuh-rawth.

Ashtoreth: *Ash*-toe-reth.

Ashurbanipal: *As*-shure-***bah***-nee-pahl.

Asia: *Ay*-zha.

Asshur: *Ash*-er.

Assyria: Uh-*sear*-ee-uh.

Assyrians: Uh-*sear*-ee-unz.

Astarte: A-*star*-tee (first *A* as in *had*).

Athaliah: Ath-uh-*lye*-uh.

Athenians: Uh-*thin*-ee-unz.

Athens: *Ath*-unz.

Attalia: At-uh-*lye*-uh.

Augustus: Aw-*gus*-tus.

Aven: *Ay*-ven.

Azaliah: Az-uh-*lye*-uh.

Azarael: *Az*-air-el or Ah-*zay*-ree-ul.

Azariah: Az-uh-*rye*-uh.

Aziliah: Az-uh-*lye*-uh.

Azmaveth: Az-*may*-veth.

Azotus: Uh-*zo*-tus.

Azriel: *Az*-rih-el.

Azzah: *Az*-uh.

— Bb —

Baal: *Bay*-ul.

Baal-berith: Bay-ul-*bee*-rith.

Baal-peor: Bay-ul-*pea*-or.

Baal-Zebub or Baal-zebub: *Bay*-ul-
    zee-bub.

Baalbek: *Bay*-ul-bek.

Baalgad: *Bay*-ul-gad.

Baali: Bay-ul-*ee* or *Bay*-ul-lye.

Baalim: Bay-uh-*leem*.

Baasha: *Bay*-uh-shuh.

Babel: *Bay*-bul.

Babylon: *Bab*-uh-lun.

Babylonia: Bab-ih-*lo*-nee-uh.

Babylonians: Bab-ih-*lo*-nee-unz.

Baca: *Bay*-kuh.

Balaam: *Bay*-lum.

Balak: *Bay*-lack.

Bani: *Bay*-nye.

Banias: *Ban*-ee-us.

Barabbas: Buh-*rab*-us.

Barachel (KJV): *Bar*-uh-kel.

Barachias: Bare-uh-*kye*-us.

Barak: *Bare*-uk.

Barakel (NIV): *Bar*-uh-kel.

barbarian: bar-*bare*-ee-un.

Barnabas: *Bar*-nuh-bus.

Barsabas: *Bar*-suh-bus.

Bartholomew: Bar-*thahl*-uh-mew.

Bartimaeus: *Bar*-tih-***me***-us or *Bar*-tih-***may***-us.

Baruch: *Bare*-uk or *Bay*-ruk.

Bb

Bashan: *Bay*-shan.

Bathsheba: Bath-*she*-buh.

Bechorath: Be-*ko*-rath.

Beelzebub: Bih-*el*-zih-bub.

Beelzebul: Bih-*el*-zih-bul.

Beer-lahai-roi: *Be*-er-luh-**hi**-roy.

Beeri: Be-*ee*-rye.

Beersheba or Beer-sheba: Beer-*she*-buh.

behemoth: *be*-heh-muth or beh-*hee*-muth.

Belial: *Be*-lih-ul.

Belshazzar: Bel-*shazz*-er.

Belteshazzar: Bel-tih-*shazz*-er.

Ben-Hadad or Ben-hadad: Ben-*hay*-dad.

Benaiah: Be-*nay*-yuh.

Benhail: Ben-*hay*-il.

Benjamin: *Ben*-juh-mun.

Beor: *Be*-or.

Berea: Buh-*ree*-uh.

Bereans: Buh-*ree*-unz.

Berechiah: Bare-uh-*kye*-uh.

Bergama: Burr-*gah*-muh.

Bernice: Ber-*nye*-see.

Berodach (KJV): Be-ro-dack.

beryl: *ber*-ul.

Bb

Beth Horon or Beth-horon: Bayth (or
Bait) *Hoe*-ron.

Beth Shemesh or Beth-shemesh: Beth-
she-mesh.

Beth-car: *Beth*-kar or Beth-*kar.*

Bethabara (KJV): *Beth*-***ab***-uh-ruh.

Bethany: *Beth*-uh-nee.

Bethaven: *Beth*-*ay*-ven.

Bethel or Beth-el: *Beth*-ul.

Bether: *Be*-ther.

Bethesda: Buh-*thez*-duh.

Bethlehem or Beth-lehem: *Beth*-lih-hem.

Bethpeor: Beth-*pea*-or.

Bethphage: *Beth*-fuh-gee.

Bethsaida: Beth-*say*-uh-duh.

Bethsaida Julias: Beth-*say*-uh-duh *Joo*-
lee-ahs.

Bethshean: Beth-*she*-un.

Bethuel: Beh-*thew*-el.

Beulah: *Bew*-lah.

Bezaleel: Bih-*zal*-ih-el.

Bildad: *Bill*-dad.

Bilhah: *Bill*-ha.

Binnui: *Bin*-you-eye.

Bithynia: Bih-*thin*-ee-uh.

blasphemer: *blas*-feem-er.

blasphemous: *blas*-fuh-mus.

blasphemy: *blas*-fuh-me.

Boanerges: *Bo*-uh-***nur***-geez.

Boaz: *Bo*-az.

Boscath: *Boz*-kath.

Bozrah: *Boz*-ruh.

Bul: Bool.

Buzi: *Bew*-zye.

— Cc —

Caesar: *See*-zer.

Caesar Augustus: *See*-zer Aw-*gus*-tus.

Caesarea: Sess-uh-*ree*-uh.

Caesarea Philippi: Sess-uh-*ree*-uh Fih-*lip*-pie or *Fil*-ih-pie.

Caiaphas: *Kay*-uh-fus or *Kye*-uh-fus.

Calah: *Kay*-luh.

calamus: *kah*-luh-mus.

Caleb: *Kay*-leb.

Calneh: *Kal*-neh.

Cambyses: Kam-*bye*-seez.

Cana: *Kay*-nuh.

Canaan: *Kay*-nun.

Canaanites: *Kay*-nun-ites.

Candace (KJV): *Kan*-duh-see.

Capernaum: Kuh-*per*-nay-um.

Caphtor: *Kaf*-tor.

Cappadocia: Kap-uh-*doe*-shuh.

Carchemish: *Kar*-key-mish.

Carmel: *Kar*-mul.

Carmelite: *Kar*-mul-ite.

carnelian (NIV): kar-*neel*-yun.

Carpus: *Kar*-pus.

cassia: *kay*-shuh.

Cauda: *Kaw*-duh.

Cedron: *See*-drun.

Cenchrea: *Sen*-kree-uh.

centurion: sen-*ture*-ee-un.

Cephas: *See*-fus.

Cerinthians: Suh-*rin*-thee-unz.

Cerinthus: Suh-*rin*-thus.

Chaldea: Kal-*dee*-uh.

Chaldeans: Kal-*dee*-unz.

Chaldees: *Kal*-deez.

Charran: *Kar*-an.

chastens: *chase*-enz.

chastisement: chas-*tize*-munt or
    chas-tuz-munt.

Cc

Chebar: *Kee*-bar.

Chedorlaomer: Ked-or-lay-*oh*-mer or
    Ked-or-*lay*-oh-mer.

Chemosh: *Kee*-mosh.

Chenaanah: Kih-*nay*-uh-nah.

Chenaniah: Ken-uh-*nee*-ah.

Cherethites: *Ker*-uh-thites.

Cherith (KJV): *Key*-rith.

cherubim: *chair*-uh-bim.

Chileab: *Kil*-ee-ab.

Chilion: *Kil*-ee-on.

Chinnereth (KJV): *Kin*-eh-reth or
    Chin-eh-reth.

Chisleu: *Kiss*-loo.

Chittim: *Kit*-tim.

Chloe: *Klo*-ee.

Chorazin: Ko-*ray*-zin.

chrysolyte: *kris*-uh-lite.

Chushai: *Koo*-shy.

Chuza: *Koo*-za.

cieled: seeld.

Cilicia: Sih-*lish*-ih-uh.

Clauda: *Claw*-duh.

Claudius Caesar: *Claw*-dee-us *See*-zer.

Claudius Lysias: *Claw*-dee-us *Liss*-ee-us.

Cleopas: *Klee*-uh-pass.

Cleophas: *Klee*-oh-fus.

Clopas: *Klo*-pus.

Colossae or Colosse: Kuh-*lahss*-ee.

Colossians: Kuh-*losh*-unz.

Coniah: Ko-*nye*-uh.

Corban: *Kor*-bun.

Corinth: *Kor*-inth.

Corinthians: Ko-*rin*-thee-unz (*th* as in *thin*).

Cornelius: Kor-*neel*-yus.

Crescens: *Kress*-enz.

Crete: Kreet.

Crispus: *Kris*-pus.

Cushi: *Koo*-shy.

Cuthah: *Kyew*-thuh.

Cyprian: *Sip*-ree-un.

Cyprus: *Sigh*-prus.

Cyrene: Sigh-*ree*-nee.

Cyrenians: Sigh-*ree*-nee-unz.

Cyrenius (KJV): Sigh-*ree*-nee-us.

Cyrus: *Sigh*-russ.

— Dd —

Dagon: *Day*-gon.

Dalmanutha: Dal-muh-*new*-thuh.

Dalmatia: Dal-*may*-shuh.

Damaris: *Dam*-uh-ris.

Damascus: Duh-*mass*-kus.

darics: *dare*-iks.

Darius: Duh-*rye*-us.

Deborah: *Deb*-uh-ruh.

Decapolis: Dee-*cap*-uh-lis.

Delaiah: Dee-*lay*-yuh.

Delilah: Dih-*lye*-luh.

Delphi: *Del*-fie.

Demas: *Dee*-mus.

Demetrius: Deh-*mee*-tree-us.

denarii: dih-*nare*-ee-ee or
     dih-*nare*-ee-eye.

denarius: dih-*nare*-ee-us.

Derbe: *Der*-be.

Deuteronomy: Due-ter-*ahn*-uh-me.

Diblaim: Dib-*lay*-im.

Didymus: *Did*-uh-mus.

Dionysius: Dye-oh-*nish*-ih-us.

Diotrephes: Dye-*ot*-rih-feez.

Dothan: *Doe*-thun (*th* as in *thin*).

Drusilla: Drew-*sil*-lah.

Dura: *Dur*-uh.

— Ee —

Ebal: *Ee*-bull.

Ebed-melech or Ebed-melek: Ee-bed-*mee*-lek.

Ebenezer: *Eb*-en-*ee*-zer.

Ecbatana: Ek-buh-*tahn*-uh.

Ecclesiastes: Ik-*leez*-ee-*as*-teez.

Edom: *Ee*-dum.

Edomites: *Ee*-dum-ites.

Egypt: *Ee*-jipt.

Egyptians: Ee-*jip*-shuns.

Ehud: *Ee*-hud.

Ekron: *Ek*-run.

El Bethel or El-beth-el: El-*beth*-ul.

Elah: *Ee*-lah.

Elam: *Ee*-lum.

Elamites: *Ee*-luh-mites.

Elasah: *El*-ah-sah.

Elath: *Ee*-lath.

Eleazar: El-ih-*ay*-zar or Ee-lih-*ay*-zar.

Eli: *Ee*-lye.

Eliab: Ee-*lye*-ab.

Eliah: Ee-*lye*-ah.

Eliakim: Ee-*lye*-uh-kim.

Eliam: Ih-*lye*-am.

Elias: Ee-*lye*-us.

Eliashib: Ee-*lye*-uh-shib.

Eliezer: El-ih-*ee*-zer.

Elihu: Ih-*lye*-hew.

Elijah: Ee-*lye*-juh.

Elim: *Ee*-lim.

Elimelech or Elimelek: Ee-*lim*-eh-leck.

Eliphaz: *El*-ih-faz.

Elisabeth: Ih-*lih*-suh-beth.

Elisha: Ee-*lye*-shuh.

Elishama: Ee-*lish*-uh-muh.

Elizabeth: Ih-*lih*-zuh-beth.

Elkanah: *El*-kuh-nuh or El-*kay*-nuh.

Elnathan: El-*nay*-thun (*th* as in *thin*).

Eloi, Eloi, lama sabachthani (Aramaic, KJV):
    Ee-*lo*-eye, Ee-*lo*-eye, *lah*-mah suh-*back*-
    thuh-nee.

Eloi, Eloi, lemasabachthani (Aramaic, NIV):
    Ee-*lo*-eye, Ee-*lo*-eye, *leh*-mah suh-*back*-
    thuh-nee.

Elul: *Ee*-lull or Eh-*lool*.

Elymas: *El*-ih-mass.

Emmanuel: Ee-*man*-you-el.

Emmaus: Em-*may*-us.

En Eglaim or En-eglaim: En-*egg*-lay-im.

En Gedi or En-gedi: En-*gee*-dye (*g* as in
   get) or En-*geh*-dee (*g* as in *get*).

Endor: *En*-dor.

enmity: *en*-mut-ee.

Enoch: *Ee*-nock.

Enos (KJV): *Ee*-nuss.

Enosh: *Ee*-nosh.

En Rogel or En-rogel: En-*ro*-gel
   (*g* as in *get*).

Epaenetus (KJV): Ee-*pea*-nee-tus.

Epaphras: *Ep*-uh-frass.

Epaphroditus: Ee-*paf*-ro-**dye**-tus.

Epenetus (NIV): Ee-*pea*-nee-tus.

ephah: *ee*-fah.

Ephesians: Ee-*fee*-zhunz.

Ephesus: *Ef*-uh-sus.

ephod: *ee*-fod.

Ephphatha (Aramic): *Ef*-uh-thuh.

Ephraim: *Ee*-fray-im.

Ephraimites: *Ee*-fray-im-ites.

Ephratah: *Ef*-rah-tah.

Ephrath: *Ef*-rath.

Ephrathite: *Ef*-ruh-thite.

Ephron: *Ee*-fron.

Epicureans: Ep-ih-kew-*ree*-unz or Ep-ih-
cure-ee-unz.

epistles: ee-*pis*-uls.

Erastus: Ee-*rass*-tus.

Esaias (KJV): Ee-*zay*-us.

Esarhaddon or Esar-haddon: Ee-sar-
had-un.

Esau: *Ee*-saw.

escheweth (KJV): ess-*shoe*-ith.

Esek: *Ee*-sek.

Eshtaol: *Esh*-tuh-oll.

Etham: *Ee*-thum.

Ethanim: *Eth*-uh-nim.

Ethbaal: Eth-*bay*-ul.

Ethiopia: Ee-thee-*oh*-pea-uh (*th* as in *thin*).

Ethiopians: Ee-thee-*oh*-pea-unz (*th* as in
thin).

Eunice: You-*nye*-see or *You*-nis.

eunuch: *you*-nick.

Euodia (NIV): You-*oh*-dee-uh.

Euodias (KJV): You-*oh*-dee-us.

Euphrates: You-*fray*-teez.

exhortation: eks-or-*tay*-shun.

Ezekiel: Ee-*zeek*-ee-ul or Ee-*zeek*-yul.

Ezion Geber or Eziongeber: *Ee*-zih-on-

gee-ber (*g* as in *get*).

Eziongaber (KJV): *Ee*-zih-on-*gay*-ber (*g* as in *get*).

Ezra: *Ez*-ruh.

— Ff —

Felix: *Fee*-licks.

Festus: *Fes*-tus.

firkins: *fir*-kuns.

fornication: for-neh-*kay*-shun.

frankincense: *frank*-in-sense.

— Gg —

Gaash: *Gay*-ash.

Gabbatha (Hebrew/ Aramaic): *Gab*-buh-thuh.

Gabriel: *Gay*-bree-ul.

Gad: *Gad* (*a* as in *bad*).

Gadarenes: *Gad*-uh-reens.

Gadites: *Gad*-ites.

Gaius: *Gay*-us.

Galatia: Guh-*lay*-shuh.

Galatians: Guh-*lay*-shunz.

Galeed: *Gal*-ee-ed.

Galileans: Gal-uh-*lee*-unz.

Galilee: *Gal*-uh-lee.

Gallio: *Gal*-ee-oh.

Gamaliel: Guh-*may*-lih-ul or Guh-*may*-
    lee-al.

Gg

Gath: Gath.

Gath Hepher or Gath-hepher: Gath-
    hee-fer.

Gaza: *Gay*-zuh.

Geba: *Gee*-buh (*G* as in *get*).

Gedaliah: *Ged*-uh-*lye*-uh (*G* as in *get*).

Gehazi: Geh-*hay*-zye (*G* as in *get*).

Gemariah: Gem-uh-*rye*-uh (*G* as in *get*).

Gennesaret: Geh-*ness*-uh-ret
    (*G* as in *get*).

Gentiles: *Jen*-tiles.

Gerar: *Gear*-ar (*G* as in *get*).

Gerasenes: *Gur*-uh-seenz.

Gergesenes: *Gur*-guh-seenz.

Gerizim: *Gare*-ih-zeem or Guh-*rye*-zim.

Gershom: *Gur*-shom.

Gershon: *Gur*-shun.

Geshem: *Gee*-shem (*G* as in *get*).

Geshur: *Gee*-shur (*G* as in *get*).

Gethsemane: Geth-*sem*-uh-nee
   (*G* as in *get*).

Gezer: *Gee*-zer (*G* as in *get*).

Gibbethon: *Gib-b*eh-thon (*G* as in *get*).

Gibeah: *Gib*-ee-uh (*G* as in *get*).

Gibeon: *Gib*-ee-un (*G* as in *get*).

Gideon: *Gid*-ee-un (*G* as in *get*).

Gihon: *Guy*-hahn.

Gilalai: *Gill*-ah-lye.

Gilboa: Gil-*bo*-uh (*G* as in *get*).

Gilead: *Gil*-ee-ud (*G* as in *get*).

Gilgal: *Gil*-gal (*G* as in *get*).

Giloh: *Guy*-lo (*G* as in *get*).

Gilonite: *Guy*-lo-nite (*G* as in *get*).

Ginath: *Guy*-nath.

Girgashites: *Gur*-guh-shites.

Gittah-hepher (KJV): *Git*-ah-***hee***-fer
   (*G* as in *get*).

Gittite: *Git*-ite (*G* as in *get*).

Golgotha: *Gahl*-guh-thuh.

Goliath: Go-*lye*-uth.

Gomorrah: Guh-*more*-uh.

Goshen: *Go*-shen.

Gozan: *Go*-zan.

Grecians: *Gree*-shunz.

Gg

— Hh —

Habakkuk: Huh-*back*-kuk.

Habaziniah or Habazziniah: Hab-uh-zih-*nye*-uh.

habergeons (KJV): *hab*-er-junz.

Habor: *Hay*-bor.

Hachaliah (KJV): Hack-uh-*lye*-uh.

Hachilah (KJV): Hah-*kye*-lah.

Hadad: *Hay*-dad.

Hadassah: Huh-*das*-suh.

Hades: *Hay*-deez.

Hagar: *Hay*-gar.

Haggai: *Hag*-eye or *Hag*-ay-eye.

Hai: *Hay*-eye.

Hakaliah (NIV): Hack-uh-*lye*-uh.

Hakilah (NIV): Hah-*kye*-lah.

Halah: *Hay*-luh.

Halak: *Hay*-lak.

Haman: *Hay*-mun.

Hamath: *Hay*-muth.

Hammedatha: Ham-meh-*day*-thuh.

Hammelech: *Ham*-muh-lek.

Hamutal: Hah-*mu*-tal.

Hanameel (KJV): *Han*-uh-meel.

Hanamel (NIV): *Han*-uh-mel.

Hanan: *Hay*-nuhn.

Hanani: Huh-*nay*-nye.

Hananiah: Han-uh-*nye*-uh.

Hannah: *Han*-nuh.

Haran (KJV): *Hare*-un.

Harhas: *Har*-haz.

Harod: *Hay*-rod.

Harosheth: Huh-*ro*-sheth.

Harran (NIV): *Hare*-un.

Hashabiah: Hash-uh-*bye*-uh.

Hashbadana or Hashbaddanah: Hash-*bad*-uh-nuh.

Hashum: *Hay*-shum.

Hatach (KJV): *Hay*-tak.

Hathak (NIV): *Hay*-thak.

Hazael: *Haz*-ay-el.

Hazor: *Hay*-zor.

Heber: *Hee*-ber.

Hebron: *Hee*-brun or *Heb*-run.

Heldai: *Hel*-day-eye.

Helem: *Hee*-lim.

Heli: *Hee*-lye.

Hellenistic: Heh-leh-*nis*-tic.

Henadad: *Hen*-uh-dad.

Hh

Hephzibah: *Hef*-zih-bah.
heresy: *hare*-uh-see.
Hermes: *Her*-meez.
Hermon: *Her*-mun.
Hermonites: *Her*-mun-ites.
Herod: *Hare*-ud.
Herodians: Heh-*ro*-dee-unz.
Herodias: Heh-*ro*-dee-us.
Hezekiah: Hez-ih-*kye*-uh.
Hezron: *Hezz*-ron.
Hiddekel: *Hid*-deh-kel.
Hierapolis: Hi-er-*ap*-oh-lis.
Hilkiah: Hill-*kye*-uh.
Hillel: *Hill*-el.
Hinnom: *Hin*-num.
Hiram: *Hi*-rum.
Hittites: *Hit*-ites or *Hit*-tites.
Hivites: *Hi*-vites.
Hodaviah: *Ho*-duh-**vie**-uh.
Hodiah (NIV): Ho-dye-uh.
Hodijah (KJV): Ho-*dye*-juh.
Hophni: *Hoff*-nye.
Horeb: *Ho*-reb.
Horonaim: Hor-oh-**nay**-im.
Horonite: *Hor*-oh-nite.

Hosea: Ho-*zay*-uh.

Hoshea: Ho-*shay*-uh.

Huldah: *Hul*-duh.

Hushai: *Hoo*-shy.

Hymenaeus: Hi-meh-*nee*-us.

hyssop: *hiss*-up.

— Ii —

Ichabod: *Ik*-uh-bod or *Ike*-uh-bod.

Iconium: Eye-*ko*-nee-um.

Iddo: *Id*-doe.

Idumaea or Idumea: Id-you-*me*-uh.

Igdaliah: Ig-duh-*lye*-uh.

Illyricum: Il-*lear*-ih-kum.

Imlah: *Im*-luh.

Immanuel: Ih-*man*-you-el.

iniquities: in-*ik*-wu-teez.

Irijah: Eye-*rye*-juh.

Isaac: *Eye*-zuk.

Isaiah: Eye-*zay*-uh.

Iscah: *Is*-kah.

Iscariot: Iss-*care*-ee-ut.

Ish-Bosheth or Ish-bosheth: Ish-*bo*-sheth.

Ishi: Ish-*eye* or *Ish*-eye.

Ishmael: *Ish*-may-el.

Ishmaelites (NIV): *Ish*-may-el-ites.

Ishmeelites (KJV): *Ish*-me-el-ites.

Israel: *Iz*-ray-el.

Israelites: *Iz*-ray-el-ites.

Issachar: *Izz*-uh-kar.

Ithamar: *Ith*-uh-mar.

Ituraea or Iturea: It-you-*ree*-uh.

—Jj—

Jaazaniah: Jay-ah-zuh-*nye*-uh.

Jabbok: *Jab*-uck.

Jabesh: *Jay*-besh.

Jabesh Gilead or: *Jay*-besh-***gil***-ee-ud.

Jabesh-gilead

Jabin: *Jay*-bin.

jacinth: *jay*-sinth.

Jacob: *Jay*-kub.

Jael: *Jay*-ul.

Jahaziel: Juh-*hay*-zee-el.

Jairus: *Jye*-rus or *Jay*-ih-rus.

Jakeh: *Jay*-keh.

Jamin: *Jay*-min.

Japheth: *Jay*-feth.

Jasher: *Jay*-sher.

Jebus: *Jee*-bus.

Jebusites: *Jeb*-yuh-sites.

Jechonias (KJV): *Jek*-oh-**nye**-us.

Jecoliah: Jek-oh-*lye*-uh.

Jeconiah (NIV): *Jek*-oh-**nye**-uh.

Jedaiah: Jeh-*day*-yah.

Jedidah: Jee-*dye*-duh.

Jedidiah: Jed-ih-*dye*-uh.

Jeduthun: Jeh-*doo*-thun.

Jehoaddan: Jee-*ho*-ud-dan.

Jehoahaz: Jeh-*ho*-uh-haz.

Jehoash (KJV): Jeh-*ho*-ash.

Jehoiachin: Jeh-*hoy*-uh-kin.

Jehoiada: Jee-*hoy*-uh-duh.

Jehoiakim: Jeh-*hoy*-uh-kim.

Jehoram: Jeh-*ho*-rum.

Jehoshaphat: Jeh-*hosh*-uh-fat.

Jehosheba: Jee-*hosh*-uh-buh.

Jehoshua: Jee-*hosh*-you-uh.

Jehovah-jireh: Jeh-*ho*-vuh-*jye*-ruh.

Jehozadak: Jeh-*hawz*-uh-dak.

Jehu: *Jay*-hew.

Jehudi: Jee-*hew*-dye.

Jephthae or Jephthah: *Jef*-thuh
    (*th* as in *thin*).

Jephunneh: Jeh-*fun*-eh.

Jerahmeel: Jee-*rah*-me-el.

Jeremiah: Jair-uh-*my*-uh.

Jeremias (KJV): Jair-uh-*my*-us.

Jericho: *Jair*-ih-co.

Jeroboam: Jair-uh-*bo*-um.

Jeroham: Jee-*ro*-ham.

Jerub-Baal or Jerubbaal: Jair-uh-*bay*-ul.

Jerusalem: Juh-*roo*-suh-lem.

Jeshua: *Jesh*-you-uh.

Jesse: *Jess*-ee.

Jethro: *Jeth*-ro.

Jezebel: *Jez*-uh-bel.

Jezreel: *Jez*-ree-el or *Jez*-reel.

Jezreelite: *Jez*-ree-el-ite.

Jezreelitess: *Jez*-ree-el-*ite*-ess.

Joab: *Jo*-ab.

Joah: *Jo*-uh.

Joahaz: *Jo*-ah-haz.

Joanna: Jo-*an*-nuh.

Joash (NIV): *Jo*-ash.

Jochebed: *Jock*-eh-bed.

Johanan: Jo-*hay*-nan.

Jonadab: *Jon*-uh-dab.

Jonah: *Jo*-nuh.

Jonas (KJV): *Jo*-nus.

Jonathan: *Jon*-uh-thun.

Joppa: *Jop*-uh.

Joram: *Jo*-ram.

Jordan: *Jor*-dun.

Josedech (KJV): *Jahss*-uh-dek.

Joses (KJV): *Jo*-sez.

Joshua: *Josh*-yew-uh.

Josiah: Jo-*sigh*-uh.

Jotham: *Jo*-thum.

Jozabad: *Joz*-ah-bad.

Jozadak (NIV): *Joz*-uh-dak.

Judaea (KJV): Joo-*dee*-uh.

Judah: *Joo*-duh.

Judaism: *Joo*-duh-izz-um or *Joo*-day-
    izz-um.

Judas: *Joo*-dus.

Judea: Joo-*dee*-uh.

Judean: Joo-*dee*-un.

Julius: *Joo*-lee-us.

Junia: *Joo*-nih-uh.

Jupiter: *Joo*-puh-ter.

Juttah: *Jut*-tah.

Jj

— Kk —

Kadesh Barnea or: *kay*-desh-***bar***-nee-uh.
Kadesh-barnea

Kadmiel: *Kad*-mih-el.

Kandake (NIV): Kan-duh-key

Kareah: Kah-*ree*-uh.

Karkor: *Kar*-kor.

Kedar: *Kee*-dar.

Kedesh-naphtali (KJV): *Kee*-desh-***naf***-tuh-lye.

Kelita: *Kel*-ih-tuh.

Kenaz: *Kee*-naz.

Kenezite or **Kenizzite:** *Ken*-ez-ite or *Ken*-uh-zite.

Kenite: *Ken*-ite.

Kerioth: *Kee*-rih-oath.

Kerith (NIV): *Kee*-rith.

Keturah: Keh-*too*-ruh.

Kidron: *Kid*-ron.

Kinnereth (NIV): *Kin*-*n*eh-reth

Kiriath Jearim (NIV): *Kir*-jath-***jee***-uh-rim
   or
   -jee-***ay***-rim.

Kirjath-jearim (KJV): *Kir*-jath-***jee***-uh-rim or

-jee-*ay*-rim.

Kishon: *Kye*-shon.

Kohath: *Ko*-hath.

Kohathite: *Ko*-hath-ite.

Korah: *Ko*-rah.

Korahites: *Ko*-rah-ites.

— Ll —

Laban: *Lay*-bun.

Laish: *Lay*-ish.

Lamech: *Lay*-mek.

Lamentations: Lam-en-*tay*-shunz.

Laodicea: Lay-*odd*-uh-**see**-uh.

Laodiceans: Lay-*odd*-uh-*see*-unz.

Lapidoth or Lappidoth: *Lap*-ih-doth.

lasciviousness: luh-*sih*-vee-us-nuss.

Lasea: Lay-*see*-uh.

Lazarus: *Laz*-uh-rus.

Lebanon: *Leb*-uh-nun.

Lemuel: *Lem*-you-el.

Levi: *Lee*-vye.

leviathan: luh-*vye*-uh-thun.

Levites: *Lee*-vites.

Levitical: Leh-*vit*-ih-kul.

Kk
Ll

Leviticus: Leh-*vit*-ih-kus.
Libertines (KJV): *Lib*-er-teens.
Libnah: *Lib*-nuh.
lintel (KJV): *lint*-ul.
Lo-Ammi or Loammi: Lo-*am*-my.
Lois: *Lo*-is.
Lo-Ruhamah or Loruhamah: *Lo*-roo-**hah**-muh.
Lucifer (KJV): *Loo*-sih-fur.
Lucius: *Loo*-shus.
Luz: Luzz.
Lycaonia: *Lik*-uh-**oh**-nih-uh.
Lydda: *Lid*-uh.
Lydia: *Lid*-ee-uh.
Lysanias: Lye-*say*-nih-us.
Lysias: *Lis*-ee-us.
Lystra: *Liss*-truh.

Ll
Mm

— Mm —

Maacah (KJV): *May*-uh-kuh.
Maai: May-*ay*-eye.
Maakah (NIV): *May*-uh-kuh.
Maaseiah: May-uh-*see*-yuh.
Macedonia: Mass-eh-*doe*-nee-uh.

Macedonians: Mass-eh-*doe*-nee-uns.

Machir (KJV): *May*-ker.

Machpelah: Mack-*pea*-luh.

Magadan (NIV): *Mag*-uh-dan.

Magdala (KJV): *Mag*-duh-luh.

Magdalene: *Mag*-duh-leen or Mag-duh-
   lee-nee.

Magi (NIV): *May*-jye or *Madge*-eye.

Mahanaim: May-hah-*nay*-im.

Maher-Shalal-Hash-Baz or: *May*-her-
   shal-al-**hash**-bas.

Maher-shalal-hash-baz

Mahlon: *Mah*-lon.

Makir (NIV): *May*-ker.

Malachi: *Mal*-uh-kye.

Malchiah (KJV): Mal-*kye*-uh.

Malchus: *Mal*-kus.

malefactors (KJV): *mal*-ih-fac-ters.

Malkijah (NIV): Mal-kye-juh.

Malta (NIV): Moll-tuh.

Mamre: *Mam*-ree.

Manaen: *Man*-uh-en.

Manasseh: Muh-*nass*-uh.

maneh (KJV): *may*-neh.

Manoah: Muh-*no*-uh.

Mm

Maon: Muh-*own.*

Marah: *Mah*-ruh.

Marduk (NIV): *Mar*-duke.

maschil or maskil: mass-*kill.*

Massah: *Mass*-uh.

Matri: *May*-try.

Mattan: *Mat*-an.

Mattaniah: Mat-tuh-*nye*-uh.

Matthew: *Math*-you.

Matthias: Muh-*thigh*-us (*th* as in *thin*).

Mattithiah: Mat-tih-*thigh*-uh.

Mazzaroth (KJV): *Maz*-uh-rahth.

Medes: Meeds.

Media: *Meed*-ee-uh.

Mediterranean: *Med*-uh-tuh-**ray**-nee-un.

Megiddo: Muh-*gid*-doe (*g* as in *get*).

Melchiah (KJV): Mel-*kye*-uh.

Melchisedec or Melchizedek: Mel-*kiz*-
eh-dek.

Melita (KJV): *Mel*-ih-tuh.

Melzar (KJV): *Mel*-zar.

Menahem: *Men*-uh-hem.

Mene Mene: *Me*-nee, *Me*-nee,

Tekel Parsin (NIV): *Tee*-kel, Par-sin

MENE MENE TEKEL UPHARSIN (KJV):

Mm

Me-nee, *Me*-nee, *Tee*-kel, You-far-sin

Mephibosheth: Meh-*fib*-oh-sheth.

Merari: Muh-*ray*-rye.

Mercurius: Mur-*koo*-ri-us.

Meremoth: *Mehr*-ee-moth.

Meribah: *Mehr*-ih-buh.

Merodach (KJV): Me-ro-dak.

Mesha: *Me*-shuh.

Meshach: *Me*-shack.

Meshullam: Me-*shul*-am.

Mesopotamia : *Mes*-uh-puh-**tay**-me-uh.

Messiah: Meh-*sigh*-uh.

Messias (KJV): Mes-*sigh*-us.

mete: meet.

Methuselah: Muh-*thoo*-zuh-luh

  (*th* as in *thin*).

Micah: *My*-kuh.

Micaiah or Michaiah: My-*kay*-uh.

Michal: *My*-kal.

Michmash (KJV): *Mik*-mash.

Michtam (Hebrew KJV): *Mik*-tam.

Midian: *Mid*-ee-un.

Midianites: *Mid*-ee-un-ites.

Mikmash (NIV): *Mik*-mash.

Miktam (NIV): *Mik*-tam.

Mm

Milcah: *Mil*-kuh.

Milcom (KJV): *Mill*-com.

Miletus: My-*lee*-tus.

Millo: *Mill*-oh.

Milkah (NIV): *Mil*-kuh.

mina (NIV): my-nuh.

Minnith: *Min*-ith.

Miriam: *Meer*-ee-um.

Mishael: *Mish*-ay-el.

Mithredath: *Mith*-ree-dath.

Mizar: *My*-zar.

Mizpah: *Miz*-pah.

Mizpeh: *Miz*-peh.

Moab: *Mo*-ab.

Moabites: *Mo*-ub-ites.

Moabitess: ***Mo***-ub-*ite*-ess.

Molech or Molek: *Mo*-lek.

Moloch (KJV): *Mo*-lock.

Morasthite (KJV): *Mo*-rass-thite.

Mordecai: *Mor*-dih-kye.

Moreh: *Mo*-reh.

Moresheth (NIV): *Mo*-resh-eth.

Moriah: Mo-*rye*-uh.

Moses: *Mo*-zes or *Mo*-zez.

murrain (KJV): *murr*-un.

Myra: *My*-ruh.

myrrh: mur.

Mysia: *Mish*-ee-uh.

— Nn —

Naamah: *Nay*-uh-muh.

Naaman: *Nay*-uh-mun.

Naamathite: *Nay*-uh-muth-ite.

Nabal: *Nay*-bull.

Naboth: *Nay*-bawth.

Nachor: *Nay*-kor.

Nadab: *Nay*-dab.

Nahor: *Nay*-hor.

Nahshon: *Nah*-shahn.

Nahum: *Nay*-hum.

Naomi: Nay-*oh*-me.

Naphtali: *Naf*-tuh-lye.

Nathan: *Nay*-thun (*th* as in *thin*).

Nathanael: Nuh-*than*-yull (*th* as in *thin*).

Nazarene: *Naz*-uh-reen.

Nazareth: *Naz*-uh-reth.

Nazarite or Nazirite: *Naz*-uh-rite.

Neapolis: Nee-*ap*-oh-lis.

Nebat: *Nee*-bat.

Nebo: *Nee*-bo.

Nebuchadnezzar: *Neb*-yuh-kud-***nez***-er.

Nebuchadrezzar (KJV): *Neb*-uh-kad-
rez-er.

Nebuzaradan: *Neb*-you-zar-*ay*-dun.

Necho: *Nee*-ko.

Negev: *Neg*-ev.

Nehemiah: *Nee*-huh-***my***-uh.

Nehushta: Nee-*hush*-tah.

Nehushtan: Nee-*hush*-tun.

Nephilim (NIV): Nef-ih-*leem*.

Nephthalim (KJV): *Nef*-thuh-lim
(*th* as in *thin*).

Neriah: Nee-*rye*-uh.

Nethaneel (KJV): Nee-*than*-ee-el
(*th* as in *thin*).

Nethanel (NIV): Nee-*than*-el (*th* as in *thin*).

Netophah: Nee-*toe*-fuh.

Netophathi (KJV): Nee-*toe*-fuh-thigh.

Netophathites (NIV): Nee-*toe*-fuh-thites.

Nicanor: Nye-*cay*-nor.

Nicodemus: *Nick*-uh-***dee***-mus.

Nicolaitans: Nik-oh-*lay*-ih-tunz.

Nicolas: *Nick*-uh-lus.

Nicopolis: Nih-*cop*-uh-lus.

Nn

Niger: *Nye*-jer.

Nimshi: *Nim*-shy.

Nineveh: *Nin*-uh-vuh.

Ninevites: *Nin*-uh-vites.

Nisan: *Nye*-san.

Noadiah: *No*-uh-***dye***-uh.

Nympha (NIV): *Nim*-fuh.

Nymphas (KJV): *Nim*-fuss.

— Oo —

Obadiah: Oh-buh-*dye*-uh.

Obed: *Oh*-bed.

Obed-Edom or Obed-edom: *Oh*-bed-
 ee-dum.

Oded: *Oh*-dead.

Olivet (KJV): *Ol*-ih-vet.

Omega: Oh-*may*-guh or Oh-*mee*-guh.

omnipotent: ahm-*nih*-poh-tent.

Omri: *Ahm*-rye.

Onesimus: Oh-*ness*-ih-muss.

Onesiphorus: *Ahn*-uh-***sif***-oh-ruhs.

Ophel: *Oh*-fel.

Ophir: *Oh*-fur.

Ophrah: *Ahf*-ruh.

Nn
Oo

Orion: Oh-*rye*-un.

Orpah: *Or*-pah.

Oshea (KJV): Oh-*shay*-uh.

Othniel: *Oth*-nih-el.

— Pp —

Padan Aram or Padan-aram: *Pay*-dan-*ay*-ram.

Pamphylia: Pam-*fill*-ee-uh.

Paphos: *Pay*-fus.

Paran: *Pare*-un.

Parmenas: *Par*-meh-nas.

Parthians: *Par*-thee-unz (*the* as in *thin*).

Patara: *Pat*-uh-ruh.

Pathros (KJV): *Path*-ros.

Patmos: *Pat*-muss.

patriarchs: *pay*-tree-arks.

Pedaiah: Peh-*day*-yuh.

Pekah: *Peek*-uh.

Pekahiah: Pek-uh-*hi*-uh.

Pelaiah: Peh-*lay*-yuh or Peh-*lye*-uh.

Pelethites: *Pel*-uh-thites.

Peniel: Peh-*nye*-el.

Peninnah: Peh-*nin*-nuh.

Oo
Pp

Pentecost: *Pent*-ih-kost.

Penuel: Pih-*noo*-el.

Perez: *Pare*-ezz.

Perga: *Per*-gah.

Pergamos (KJV): *Per*-guh-muss.

Pergamum (NIV): *Per*-guh-mum.

Perizzites: *Pare*-ih-zites.

Persia: *Per*-zhuh.

Pethor: *Pea*-thor.

Pethuel: Peth-*you*-el.

Phanuel (KJV): Fuh-*nyoo*-el.

Pharaoh: *Fare*-oh or *Fay*-ro.

Pharaoh-Nechoh: *Fay*-ro-*Nee*-ko.

Pharez (KJV): *Fare*-ezz.

Pharisees: *Fare*-ih-seez.

Pharpar: *Far*-par.

Phebe (KJV): *Fee*-be.

Phenice (NIV): Fih-*nye*-see.

Phicol or Phichol: *Fye*-kahl.

Philemon: Fih-*lee*-mun or Fye-*lee*-mun.

Philetus: Fuh-*lee*-tus.

Philippi: Fih-*lip*-pie or *Fil*-ih-pie.

Philippians: Fih-*lip*-ee-unz.

Philistia: Fuh-*liss*-tee-uh.

Philistines: Fuh-*liss*-teenz or *Fill*-us-teenz.

Pp

Phinehas: *Fin*-ee-us.

Phoebe (NIV): *Fee*-be.

Phoenicia: Fuh-*nish*-uh.

Phoenix (NIV): Fee-niks.

Phrygia: *Frij*-ee-uh.

phylacteries: fih-*lak*-ter-eez.

Pi Hahiroth or Pi-hahiroth: Pie Hah-*hi*-roth.

Pilate: *Pie*-lut.

Pisgah: *Piz*-guh.

Pisidia: Pih-*sid*-ee-uh.

Pisidian: Pih-*sid*-ee-un.

Pithom: *Pie*-thum.

Pleiades: *Plee*-uh-deez.

Pollux: *Pol*-*l*uks.

pomegranate: *pom*-ih-gran-it.

Pontius Pilate: *Pon*-shus or *Pon*-tee-us *Pie*-lut.

Pontus: *Pon*-tuss.

Porcius Festus: *Por*-she-us *Fess*-tus.

Potiphar: *Pot*-ih-far.

Potiphera or Poti-pherah: *Pot*-ih-*fee*-ruh.

potsherd: *pot*-sherd.

Praetorium: Pree-*tor*-ee-um.

Pp

Prisca: *Pris*-kuh.

Priscilla: Prih-*sil-l*uh.

privily (KJV): *prih*-vuh-lee.

Prochorus or Procorus: *Prock*-uh-rus.

propitiation (KJV): pro-*pih*-she-**ay**-shun.

proselyte (KJV): *prahss*-uh-lite.

Ptolemais: Toll-uh-*may*-us.

Puah: *Pew*-ah.

Purim: *Pew*-rim.

Puteoli: Pew-*tee*-oh-lee.

— Qq —

quaternions (KJV): kwa-*ter*-nee-unz.

Quirinius (NIV): Kwy-*rin*-ee-us.

— Rr —

Raamses (KJV): Ray-*am*-seez.

Rabbah: *Rab*-buh.

rabbi: *rab*-eye.

Rabboni: Rab-*oh*-nye.

Rabshakeh (KJV): *Rab*-she-keh or
    Rab-*shay*-keh.

Raca: *Ray*-kuh or Ray-*kah*.

Pp
Qq
Rr

Rachab (KJV): *Ray*-hab.

Rahab: *Ray*-hab.

Ramah: *Ray*-muh.

Ramathaim-zophim (KJV): *Ray*-muh-
thay-im–*zo*-fim.

Rameses (NIV): *Ram*-ih-seez.

Ramoth Gilead or: *Ray*-muth-*gil*-ee-ud.

Ramoth-gilead

Rebekah: Reh-*bek*-uh.

Rechab (KJV): *Ree*-kab.

Rechabites (KJV): *Reck*-uh-bites.

Rehoboam: Ree-huh-*boe*-um.

Rehoboth: Ree-*ho*-bahth.

Rekab (NIV): *Ree*-kab.

Rekabites (NIV): *Reck*-uh-bites.

Remaliah: Rem-uh-*lye*-uh.

Rephaim: *Ref*-ay-im.

Rephidim: *Ref*-ih-dim.

Reuben: *Roo*-ben.

Reubenites: *Roo*-ben-ites.

Reuel: *Roo*-el.

Rezin: *Ree*-zin.

Rezon: *Ree*-zun.

Rhegium: *Ree*-jih-um.

Riblah: *Rib*-luh.

Rufus: *Roo*-fus.

— Ss —

Sabaoth or sabaoth (KJV): *Sab*-ah-oth.

Sabeans: Suh-*be*-unz.

sacrilege: *sak*-rih-lej.

Sadducees: *Sad*-you-seez.

Salamis: *Sal*-uh-mis.

Salmon: *Sal*-mun.

Salome: Suh-*loh*-me.

Samaria: Suh-*mare*-ee-uh.

Samaritans: Suh-*mare*-uh-tunz.

Samothrace (NIV): Sam-oh-thrase.

Samothracia (KJV): Sam-oh-*thray*-shuh.

Samuel: *Sam*-you-el.

Sanballat: San-*bal*-ut.

Sanhedrin: *San*-huh-drun or
    San-*heed*-run.

Sapphira: Suh-*fye*-ruh.

Sarah: *Say*-ruh.

Sarai: *Seh*-rye.

Sardis: *Sar*-dis.

sardius (KJV): *sard*-ee-us.

sardonyx (KJV): sar-*dahn*-iks.

Rr
Ss

Sargon: *Sar*-gon.

Saron (KJV): *Say*-ron.

Satan: *Say*-tun.

savourest: *say*-ver-ust.

Sceva: *See*-vuh.

Scythian: *Sith*-ee-un.

seah (NIV): *seh*-ah.

Seba: *See*-buh.

Seir: *See*-ir.

Seirah (NIV): See-eye-ruh.

Seirath (KJV): See-*eye*-rath.

Selah (Hebrew): *See*-luh.

Seleucia: Seh-*loo*-shuh.

Sennacherib: Sen-*nack*-er-ib.

Sepharvaim: Sef-ar-*vay*-im.

sepulchre (KJV): *sep*-ul-kur.

Seraiah: See-*ray*-yuh or See-*rye*-uh.

seraphim: *sair*-uh-fim.

Sergius Paulus: *Ser*-jih-us *Paul*-us.

Shabbethai: *Shab*-ee-thigh.

Shadrach: *Shay*-drack or *Shad*-rack.

Shalem (KJV): *Shay*-lem.

Shallum: *Shall*-um.

Shalmaneser: Shal-mun-*ee*-zer.

Shamgar: *Sham*-gar.

Ss

Shammai: *Sham*-eye.

Shaphan: *Shay*-fan.

Shaphat: *Shay*-fat.

Shealtiel: She-*al*-tee-el.

Shear-Jashub or Shear-jashub: *She*-ar-***jah***-shub.

Sheba: *She*-buh.

Shebna: *Sheb*-nuh.

Shechaniah (KJV): Shek-uh-*nye*-uh.

Shechem: *Shee*-kem or *Shek*-em.

Shekaniah (NIV): Shek-uh-*nye*-uh.

Shelemiah: Shel-ee-*my*-uh.

Shema: *She*-muh

Shemaiah: She-*may*-yuh or Shee-*my*-uh.

Shemer: *Shee*-mer.

Sherebiah: *Sher*-ee-***bye***-uh.

Sheshbazzar: Shesh-*baz*-ar.

Shethar-Bozenai or: *She*-thar-***boz***-nye.

Shethar-boznai

Shiloh: *Shy*-lo.

Shilonite: *Shy*-lo-nite.

Shimei: *Shim*-ee-eye.

Shinar: *Shy*-nar.

Shiphrah: *Shif*-ruh.

Shishak: *Shy*-shak.

Ss

Shittim or shittim: *Shih-teem.*

Shuah: *Shoo-uh.*

Shuhite: *Shoo-hite.*

Shunammite: *Shoo-nam-ite.*

Shunem: *Shoo-nem.*

Shushan (KJV): *Shoo-shan.*

Sichem (KJV): *Sigh-kem.*

Sidon: *Sigh-dun.*

Sidonians: *Sigh-doe-nee-uns.*

Sihon: *Sigh-hun.*

Silas: *Sigh-luss.*

Siloam: Sigh-*lo*-um.

Silvanus: Sil-*vay*-nus.

Simeon: *Sim*-ee-un.

Simon: *Sigh*-mun.

Simon Barjona (KJV): *Sigh*-mun
    Bar-*joe*-nuh.

Sinai: *Sigh*-nye or *Sigh*-nay-eye.

Sisera: *Sis*-er-uh.

Sitnah: *Sit*-nuh.

Smyrna: *Smur*-nuh.

Socoh (KJV): *So*-ko.

Sodom: *Sod*-um.

Sokoh (NIV): *So*-ko.

Solomon: *Sol*-oh-mun.

Ss

Sorek: *So*-rek.

Sosthenes: *Soss*-thuh-neez.

Stephanas: *Stef*-uh-nass.

Stephen: *Stee*-ven.

Stoic (NIV): *stoe*-ik.

Stoicks (KJV): *stoe*-iks.

Succoth (KJV): *Soo*-kawth.

Suetonius: Soo-*toe*-nee-us.

Sukkoth (NIV): *Soo*-kawth.

Susa (NIV): *Soo*-suh.

Sychar: *Sigh*-kar.

synagogue: *sin*-uh-gog.

Syntyche: *Sin*-tih-key.

Syria: *Sear*-ee-uh.

Syrians (KJV): *Sear*-ee-unz.

Syro-phenician (KJV): *Sigh*-ro-fih-
  nish-un.

— Tt —

Ss
Tt

Tabeal or Tabeel: *Tay*-be-ul.

Taberah: *Tab*-eh-ruh.

tabernacle: ***tah***-burr-*nah*-kul.

Tabitha: *Tab*-ih-thuh.

Tabor: *Tay*-ber.

Tahpanhes: *Tah*-pan-heez.

Talitha cumi (Aramaic, KJV): *Tal*-ih-thuh-***koo***-my or Tuh-*lee*-thuh-***koo***-me.

Talitha koum (Aramaic, NIV): *Tal*-ih-thuh-***koom***.

Tamar: *Tay*-mer.

Tarshish: *Tar*-shish.

Tarsus: *Tar*-sus.

Tatnai (KJV): *Tat*-nye or *Tat*-eh-nye.

Tattenai (NIV): *Tat*-nye or *Tat*-eh-nye.

teil (KJV): tile.

Tekoa: Tih-*ko*-uh.

Teman: *Tee*-mun.

Temanite: *Tee*-mun-ite.

Terah: *Tare*-uh.

terebinth (NIV): *ter*-uh-binth.

Tertullus: Tur-*tull*-us.

tetrarch: *teh*-trark or *tee*-trark.

Tt

Thaddaeus: Thad-*dee*-us (*a* as in *hat*).

Tharshish (KJV): *Thar*-shish (*th* as in *thin*).

Theophilus: Thee-*ahf*-ih-luss (*th* as in *thin*).

Thessalonians: *Thess*-uh-***lo***-nee-unz (*th* as in *thin*).

Thessalonica: *Thess*-uh-lo-***nye***-kuh

(*th* as in *thin*).

Theudas: *Thoo*-dus.

Thummim: *Thum*-im (*th* as in *thin*).

Thyatira: *Thy*-uh-*tie*-ruh (*th* as in *thin*).

Tiberias: Tie-*beer*-ee-us.

Tibni: *Tib*-nye.

Tiglath-Pileser or Tiglath-pileser:
    Tig-lath-pih-*lee*-zer.

Tigris: *Tie*-griss.

Tikvah: *Tick*-vuh.

Tilgath-pilneser (KJV): *Til*-gath-
    pil-*nee*-zer.

Timnath-Heres or: *Tim*-nath-*hee*-reez.

Timnath-heres

Timnath-Serah or: *Tim*-nath-*see*-ruh.

Timnath-serah

Timon: *Tie*-mon.

Timotheus (KJV): Tih-*mo*-the-us
    (*th* as in *thin*).

Timothy: *Tim*-oh-thee (*th* as in *thin*).

Tiphsah: *Tif*-suh.

Tirshatha (KJV): Tur-*shay*-thuh.

Tirzah: *Tur*-zuh.

Tishbe: *Tish*-be.

Tishbite: *Tish*-bite.

Tt

Titus: *Tie*-tus.

Tobiah: Toe-*bye*-uh.

Tobijah: Toe-*buy*-jah.

Tohu: *Toe*-hew.

Toi (KJV): *Toe*-eye.

Tophet: *Toe*-fet.

Tou (NIV): Toe-you.

Trachonitus or Traconitus: *Trak*-oh-nye-tus.

Troas: *Tro*-az.

Trophimus: *Troff*-ih-muss.

Tychicus: *Tick*-ih-cuss.

Tyrannus: Ty-*ran*-nus.

Tyre: Tire.

— Uu —

Ulai: *You*-lye or *You*-luh-eye.

Ur: Er.

Urbane (KJV): Er-*bane*.

Urbanus (NIV): Er-ban-us.

Uri: *You*-rye.

Uriah: You-*rye*-uh.

Urijah: You-*rye*-juh.

Urim: *You*-rim.

Tt

Uu

Uzzah: *Uz*-zuh.
Uzziah: Uh-*zye*-uh.

— Vv —

Vashti: *Vash*-tie.

— Ww —

whoremongers (KJV): *hor*-mon-gerz.

— Ww —

Xerxes (NIV): *Zerk*-seez.

— Zz —

Zabdi: *Zab*-dye.
Zabulon (KJV): *Zab*-you-lon.
Zacchaeus: Zack-*key*-us.
Zaccur (KJV): *Zak*-kur.
Zachariah (KJV): Zack-uh-*rye*-uh.
Zacharias (KJV): Zack-uh-*rye*-us.
Zadok: *Zay*-dok.
Zakkur (NIV): *Zak*-kur.

Uu
Vv
Ww
Xx
Yy
Zz

Zaphenath-Paneah (NIV): *Zaf*-uh-nath-
   puh-*nee*-uh.

Zaphnath-paaneah (KJV): *Zaf*-nath-
   pay-uh-nee-uh.

Zarah or Zerah: *Zare*-uh.

Zarephath: *Zare*-uh-fath.

Zaretan (KJV): *Zare*-uh-tan.

Zarethan (NIV): *Zare*-uh-than.

Zarthan (KJV): *Zar*-than.

Zealot (NIV): *Zel*-ut.

Zebadiah: *Zeb*-uh-**dye**-uh.

Zebedee: *Zeb*-eh-dee.

Zebidah (NIV): *Zeb*-ih-duh.

Zeboim: Zeh-*bo*-im.

Zebudah (KJV): Zeh-*boo*-duh.

Zebul: *Zee*-bul.

Zebulun: *Zeb*-you-lun.

Zechariah: *Zek*-uh-**rye**-uh.

Zedekiah: Zed-uh-*kye*-uh.

Zelophehad: Zeh-*lo*-feh-had.

Zelotes (KJV): Zeh-*lo*-teez.

Zephaniah: Zef-uh-*nye*-uh.

Zeror: *Zee*-ror.

Zerubbabel: Zeh-*rub*-uh-bul.

Zeruiah: *Zer*-you-**eye**-uh.

Zz

Zeus: Zoose.

Zibiah: *Zib*-ee-uh.

Zidon (KJV): *Zye*-dun.

Zidonians (KJV): Zye-*doe*-nee-uns.

Zif (KJV): *Zif.*

Ziklag: *Zik*-lag.

Zilpah: *Zil*-pah.

Zimri: *Zim*-rye.

Zion: *Zye*-un.

Ziph: *Zif.*

Ziphites: *Zif*-ites.

Zippor: *Zip*-or.

Zipporah: Zih-*po*-ruh.

Ziv (NIV): *Ziv.*

Zoar: *Zo*-er.

Zophar: *Zo*-far.

Zophim: *Zo*-fim.

Zorah: *Zo*-ruh.

Zuph: *Zuf.*

Zz